It was an Olympic night that inspired an entire nation. The seven members of the women's gymnastics team were doing what no American team had ever done—they were fulfilling their personal quests, and America's dream, of capturing the team gold medal. With each event, the young women's indomitable spirit and talent shined. The seven athletes—Amanda Borden, Amy Chow, Dominique Dawes, Shannon Miller, Dominique Moceanu, Jaycie Phelps, and Kerri Strug—performed brilliantly as a team. Together they won gold at the 1996 Olympics; together they secured a place in Olympic history. Together they *are* the Magnificent Seven.

The MAGNIFICENT SEVEN

THE AUTHORIZED STORY OF AMERICAN GOLD

written by Nancy H. Kleinbaum

BANTAM BOOKS

NEW YORK • TORONTO • LONDON • SYDNEY • AUCKLAND

The MAGNIFICENT SEVEN

THE AUTHORIZED STORY OF AMERICAN GOLD

written by Nancy H. Kleinbaum

BANTAM BOOKS
NEW YORK • TORONTO • LONDON • SYDNEY • AUCKLAND

Dedications

To my parents, Doug and Patty; my brother, Bryan; my coach, Mary Lee Tracy; and my teammate, Jaycie.   —A.B.

To my coaches and my family.   —A.C.

With thanks to the Lord, without whose strength I don't think I could have gotten to where I am today. Also, to my coaches; Dr. William Wolf of Shady Grove Hospital; Carolyn Silby, my sports psychologist; all of my family and friends; my teammates, agents, sponsors; the media; and all my fans who believed in me throughout all these years.   *love*—D.D. "Awesome Dawesome"

To my mom, Claudia; dad, Ron; sister, Tessa; and brother, Troy, who have all been there to inspire and motivate me, to advise and console, and to laugh and cry with me. Thank you for always loving me no matter what.
To my coaches, Steve Nunno and Peggy Liddick, two of the most dedicated, hardworking, and caring coaches any athlete could ever have.
Thank you for teaching me so much more than gymnastics.
To Kittie Burris, whose generosity, love, and gentle reminders have taught me to rely on God for the strength I need both inside and outside the gym.   —S.M.

To my parents and coaches, who supported me all the way. Without them I couldn't have done it.   *with love*—D.M.

To my coach, Mary Lee Tracy; to my family; and to my best teammate, Amanda.
—J.P.

To everyone who has helped me become what I am today, and to the people of America, who have supported me through this whole Olympics, especially my mom, dad, brother, sister, aunt, and uncle, and the many coaches who have helped me along the way, especially Bela Karolyi.   *with deepest thanks*—K.S.

CONTENTS

Amanda
Borden

A M A N D A
BORDEN

VITAL STATISTICS

BIRTHDATE: MAY 10, 1977

HEIGHT AND WEIGHT: 5 FT, 3 IN, 108 LBS

HOMETOWN: CINCINNATI, OHIO

PARENTS: DOUG AND PATTY BORDEN

SIBLING: BRYAN, 22

CLUB: CINCINNATI GYMNASTICS ACADEMY

COACH: MARY LEE TRACY

BEGAN GYMNASTICS: 1984

"I'm outgoing," says team captain Amanda Borden. "I like to liven things up and make people happy."

On the evening of July 23, 1996, Amanda and her six teammates on the U.S. Olympic women's gymnastics team did exactly that. At stake? The gold medal for team competition—a medal no U.S. women's team had ever won. This year the elusive gold seemed a tantalizing possibility.

For decades the United States women's gymnastics team had trailed behind powerhouse teams from Romania and the former Soviet Union. For the 1996 Games, the teams from Romania and Russia, along with newcomer China, were expected to take home medals once again.

But for Amanda Borden and her teammates, fourth place wasn't good enough. Each team member was determined to do her absolute, ultimate best, showing the world that the American team had the talent and strength to perform under the intense Olympic pressure.

On the day of the team compulsories, Amanda recalls, she felt much more nervous than usual. As team captain, she picked up on her teammates' nervousness as well. But the athletes worked through their tension and turned in solid, dynamic performances that awed audiences and competing teams alike. By the end of the evening, the American team was in the silver medal position—right behind Russia.

Then came the optionals. In this one competition, the American athletes could cover themselves with glory or join the ranks of past U.S. teams who hadn't made the grade.

When Team USA arrived at the Georgia Dome that afternoon, they felt confident. Their terrific showing in the compulsories had helped them to relax and view their upcoming performance as just another meet. As team captain, Amanda wondered if a pep talk was in order before they began. In the end she realized that each of her teammates knew what she had to do—after all, Team USA was made up of some of the best gymnasts in the world. But Amanda did try to connect with each of them personally.

Courtesy of Borden family

At age two and a half, Amanda opened Christmas presents with her dog, Pirate. She was happy to get the toy kitchen.

THE MAGNIFICENT SEVEN

The audience in the Georgia Dome roared with approval when the women's team appeared. "I've been in front of American spectators in national competitions around the country," Amanda says, "but there had never been a crowd like the Olympic crowd. It was unbelievable how supportive they were of the U.S. team."

In the compulsories, each member of each team must demonstrate proficiency on an apparatus with identical choreography; in the optionals, the athletes have much more freedom. It's a chance to show off strengths and downplay weaknesses. And it's an opportunity for each gymnast to demonstrate creativity and flair in her favorite events. (After the 1996 Games, gymnastics compulsories will no longer be required.)

Courtesy of Borden family

Amanda and her big brother, Bryan, in 1983.

On optionals night, the first event for Team USA was the uneven parallel bars. One by one, members of the team performed their routines. The feedback from the audience was awesome, with more than eighty thousand fans shouting their approval of the team's strong showing. Three other events followed: the balance beam, the floor exercise, and the vault.

At the same time, the Russian team, the Romanians, and the Chinese were performing on apparatuses set up on the floor of the Georgia Dome. "We felt as if we were the only ones out on the floor," Amanda says. "Even my parents, who were in the stands, said all they could watch was the American team. And that's what we wanted. We had the home court advantage."

Amanda flashed a victorious smile after winning her first gold medal for her performance in the floor exercise at the 1988 AAU Junior Olympics in Kansas.

Sometimes the Romanians were ahead, sometimes the Russians. Scores judged in hundredths of a point kept pace throughout the evening. Members of each of the four teams turned in performances that alternated between awe-inspiring and groan-producing. When the American team captured the gold medal, it was the culmination of seven individual lifetimes of effort, dreams, and hope.

Some athletes start gymnastics before age seven, but it took Amanda that long to settle on her sport. Naturally athletic, she played T-ball and soccer, ice-skated, and took ballet while she was very young. When a family friend saw Amanda in a ballet recital, she noted that Amanda looked more like a gymnast than a ballerina. Inspired by Mary Lou Retton's performance at the 1984 Olympics, Amanda switched sports once more, and at last found her all-time favorite.

THE MAGNIFICENT SEVEN

Amanda's mother contacted a local gymnastics school in their hometown, Cincinnati, Ohio. The first week, Amanda took one one-hour class. That was enough to convince her coaches that she had unusual potential. She moved right away to a two-hour class three times a week, as part of the Junior Elite Testing program. High scores there meant she could be eligible for a national-level training camp.

By the age of ten, Amanda was competing at the compulsory level at meets in Ohio, Kentucky, Indiana, and Michigan. Her parents and her older brother, Bryan, were amazingly supportive, traveling with her to meets and driving her to practice, but her parents always emphasized that their main concern was that Amanda be happy in what she did. It's a Borden family belief that enjoying what you do is far more important than being number one.

Amanda won four medals at the 1990 Regionals (Level 10) held in Michigan. The other winners (from left): Kim Koch, Karin Lichey, Mandi Hinson.

When Amanda was thirteen, she realized that she had the potential to be a really good gymnast—perhaps a world-class one. With that realization came the decision to switch training centers.

Her new gym was the Cincinnati Gymnastics Academy, run by Mary Lee Tracy. "As soon as I moved to Mary Lee's, things started," Amanda says. "My parents could see it, and my coaches could see it. When I switched to a new environment, things started to move faster and faster." In fact, by 1990 Amanda qualified for the Junior Olympic Nationals in Colorado Springs.

"Mary Lee is different than a lot of coaches," Amanda declares. "She sets a great example for coaches around the coun-

Courtesy of Borden family

Amanda loved Australia and found time for a kangaroo friend when she competed in the 1994 World Championships in Brisbane.

try. She definitely gets on us, telling us to point a toe or straighten a leg, but she cares so much for us as people, and that makes all the difference. We know when she says, 'That was not a good routine,' that we shouldn't take it personally. She's just trying to make us better gymnasts. She'll still like us as people no matter what."

Tracy's approach helps Amanda perform her best, because Amanda feels as if she's striving to achieve her own goals, not her coach's. "If you feel you're doing it for someone else, it makes you nervous," Amanda explains. "Then you start messing up."

THE MAGNIFICENT SEVEN

Over the next few years, Amanda worked on honing her competition skills. Each season Amanda, her parents, and Mary Lee decided where Amanda would compete. It always depended on whether Amanda felt prepared. "If you haven't prepared well and you're not very confident, you don't want to compete," she explains. "You don't want to get in a situation where you mess up and know that it wouldn't have happened with more practice." Knowing that she could always be better with additional practice, Amanda continually strived to improve her skills. The floor exercise, uneven parallel bars, and balance beam were strong events for her. The vault was her weakness, and that bothered her. "I've never been really strong in [the vault], which is probably why I didn't like it. But I've worked on it and I've got it under control." Spending hour upon hour in the gym, doing different vaults hundreds of times, helped Amanda feel more secure. "But even if you've done it a zillion times, once you get into a competition situation, anything can happen," she says wryly.

Anything can happen in or out of a competition situation, as Amanda discovered the following year. In 1991 she came in third for her age level at an Elite-level meet in Arizona, which qualified her for her first U.S. Championships—a turning point in her career.

Amanda shared a lot of good times with teammates Jaycie Phelps and Amy Chow during the 1994 Team World Championships in Dortmund, Germany.

Crowned Finneytown High School's Homecoming Queen, Amanda posed with Homecoming King Dave Mackzum (1994).

Courtesy of Borden family

That was when the first of her major injuries occurred. Three months before the championships, she broke her elbow. Her arm was in a cast for six weeks—after which she bounced back and resumed training. As soon as she hit the gym again, she pulled a hamstring so badly that she could hardly walk—much less vault, run, do splits, or make any other move she needed for gymnastics. There was nothing to do except wait the injuries out and set her sights on the following year.

By the time her body was healthy again, Amanda was fifteen and therefore required to compete at the Senior Elite level, going up against big names such as Shannon Miller, Kim Zmeskal, and Betty Okino in the U.S. Championships in Columbus, Ohio. Coming in fifth in that meet qualified Amanda for the 1992 Olympic Trials.

The trials took place in Baltimore that year. Amanda put in the performance of her life and came in seventh all-around. Because seven girls would qualify for the team, it seemed clear that Amanda would be part of Team USA in Barcelona in 1992.

"I never dreamed I'd qualify for the Olympics," Amanda says. "I was just doing gymnastics because I enjoyed it." But after the trials, she realized how much she wanted to go, to be a part of history. At the age of fifteen, she was at the pinnacle of her career.

However, Barcelona was a dream that never materialized. For various reasons outside Amanda's control, it was decided to send to the 1992 Games two other athletes who had been injured and had not competed at the trials. Amanda and Kim Kelly were bumped off the team. For Amanda, from the height of her career to her lowest point was a short, fast trip.

But Amanda was only fifteen, after all. Young and resilient, she could have another shot at the Olympics one day. In the meantime, there were plenty of challenges to keep her involved and on her toes in her chosen sport.

In 1993 she competed in the U.S. Championships and finished fourth. Somehow she also found the time to compete in the American Classic in Salt Lake City; the McDonald's American Cup in Orlando; the Hilton Challenge in Los Angeles; the Chunichi Cup in Nagoya, Japan; the Tokyo Cup; and the World Championships in Birmingham, England, as an alternate. Whew!

Traveling was a fantastic learning experience, Amanda found. Comparing other countries with America made her appreciate just how great things are here. "I love meeting people," she says. "I've developed great relationships with coaches, friends, and teammates all around this country and the world." Still, Australia, which she visited in 1994 as part of the American team for the World Gymnastics Championships, remains her favorite foreign country—because "it's so much like America!"

In 1994 Amanda had terrific meets at the World Gymnastics Championships, the Team World Championships in Dortmund, Germany, the U.S. Classic in Palm Springs, California, and several other competitions that kept her living out of a suitcase. She was turning in great performances and building a solid reputation as a tough, graceful competitor. And she was already looking toward trying to qualify for the 1996 Olympic team.

Courtesy of Mary Lee Tracy

Amanda and Jaycie Phelps took a little break after one of their training sessions at the 1996 Olympics.

The Borden family in 1995. Mr. Borden is at Amanda's right, Mrs. Borden in the back, along with Amanda's brother, Bryan. Aunts and uncles made up the rest of the group.

Courtesy of Borden family

An important decision had to be made, however. Earlier in the year, Amanda had applied to and been accepted at the University of Georgia, which had awarded her a gymnastics scholarship. But if she planned to shoot for the Olympics, college would have to be put on hold. "It was a huge decision," she says. "My parents and Mary Lee felt I had to make it by myself. I had to do what I wanted to do." Amanda was already eighteen years old. This was probably her last shot at the Olympics. She decided to gamble on making the Olympic team and regretfully postponed academics.

The year 1995 took its toll on her physically. She graduated from Cincinnati's Finneytown High School, a straight-A student and Homecoming Queen. With school over, she could concentrate full-time on her gymnastics training. But a broken toe sidelined her for eight weeks, keeping her out of the U.S. Championships, the World Championship trials, and the World Championships.

Later that year, while practicing for an exhibition, she sprained her ankle and had to miss another important competition. She set her sights on 1996, once again impatiently waiting out her injuries.

By the spring of 1996, Amanda was eager to compete. But while in training for the American Classic in Tulsa, she broke another bone—this time a metacarpal in her hand. So much for that competition. A less determined athlete might have been ready to give up. But Amanda, with the support of her family and coaches, made the decision to stick with her dream. About eight weeks before the Olympic Trials, she got the go-ahead to compete.

On the beam at the 1996 Olympics, Amanda nailed a tumbling pass.

Coach Mary Lee put Amanda and her training partner (and fellow Olympic team member) Jaycie Phelps on an accelerated training schedule. Since they would compete on a Sunday in the trials, the girls began working out on Sundays (as well as on other days) to get their bodies in sync. To Amanda, training with Jaycie made all the difference. For the 1992 Olympic Trials, she had trained alone and had found it very difficult. But Amanda and Jaycie supported and challenged each other during the intensive training sessions.

"I did have moments when I thought, *Why am I doing this? I hate this! It's so hard!*" Amanda says. "But then I'd finish, and I'd feel exhausted, like I couldn't have done better, couldn't have given any more. I loved the feeling of giving it my all." That was the feeling that kept her going through years of injuries, through the disappointment of not making the Barcelona team, through the day-in, day-out training.

Amanda showed some awesome moves during her floor exercise at the 1996 Olympics.

"With Jaycie, we said, 'Either we both make it, or neither of us should make it,'" Amanda says. "We had trained so hard together, given it everything we could. We couldn't have done more—and Mary Lee was giving us everything she had too. The trials were very emotional for us all."

That emotion and hard work paid off. Both girls made the team. Amanda feels there's a misconception about her career—that if she hadn't made the Olympic team for the second time, her years of effort would have been a waste. She disagrees. "I would never say that the Olympics are the only goal for me. There are so many things I've accomplished and so many things I've done besides making the team."

But, happily, she did make the team and was honored by her teammates when they elected her team captain. Basically the team captain acts as a go-between if there are problems between athletes and coaches. "Luckily, I didn't have to deal with any of that," Amanda says with relief. "We had no problems whatsoever." She also acted as the pep squad, cheering on her teammates if they felt nervous.

For security, the U.S. women's gymnastics team stayed in a fraternity house at Atlanta's Emory University, instead of at the Olympic Village. For Amanda and roommate Jaycie, the first couple of days were hard. Both young women are more comfortable on their home ground, surrounded by their friends and family. But they quickly adjusted and soon felt confident that they could put in their best work even though they were so far from home. They were proved right.

"We made history!" Amanda says of that night in July when the American team's score edged out the Russians'. "For another couple of years I don't think anyone will forget the gymnastics team. It's unbelievable!"

For Amanda, it was the achievement of a young lifetime. The injuries are forgotten, as are past disappointments. Now she remembers the joy of giving her all and the deep satisfaction of knowing she was part of a team that made a difference: the *first* women's gymnastics team from America to take home the gold.

And in the future? Amanda's life will never be the same. There will be ticker-tape parades in her hometown. There will be guest appearances, interviews, perhaps endorsements. Then college, definitely. Amanda's older brother, Bryan, is studying physical therapy, and Amanda would like to pursue that career as well. "I'd like to have a positive impact on kids' lives," she says seriously. "I've been blessed with so many wonderful things. I'd like to pass on my knowledge. Working with athletes is important to me, so physical therapy is a natural."

What comes naturally to Amanda Borden, gold medal champion, is an ability to give her all—whether to her sport, to her teammates, or to her future career.

Duomo/David Madison

AMY
CHOW

★

VITAL STATISTICS

BIRTHDATE: MAY 15, 1978
HEIGHT AND WEIGHT: 5 FT, 1 IN, 90 LBS
HOMETOWN: SAN JOSE, CALIFORNIA
PARENTS: NELSON AND SUSAN CHOW
SIBLING: KEVIN, 16
CLUB: WEST VALLEY GYMNASTICS SCHOOL
COACHES: MARK YOUNG, DIANE AMOS
BEGAN GYMNASTICS: 1981

"I really just hoped to make the finals," says Amy Chow. "Winning the [silver] medal was just . . . extra."

The 1996 Olympics were certainly Amy's time for "extras" and a time for firsts: the first gold medal for the U.S. women's gymnastics team, the first time an Asian American had been part of such a team, and Amy's personal first—her individual silver Olympic medal for her performance on the uneven parallel bars.

Of the three accomplishments, though, contributing to the team effort was perhaps the most rewarding for Amy. "It was terrific just to be on the team," she says. "And when we won the team gold, I couldn't believe it. We knew we could do it, but when it finally happened, it was absolutely unreal."

If one word could sum up Amy Chow, it might be *contradiction*. She's a highly visible athlete in what is perhaps the most publicized Olympic sport, but she shuns publicity. Happy to contribute to and support her team, she's an extremely accomplished individual who won her own silver medal on the uneven parallel bars. Though she has reached the pinnacle of success in her chosen sport, she has also dived competitively and ranks playing classical piano only a short notch below gymnastics. Born in America, she is far from being a typical American teenager. She is Amy Chow, gold medal champion.

Amy's mother, Susan, was born in Hong Kong. Amy's father, Nelson, was born in Canton, China. Each emigrated to America to pursue university studies. They met, married, and started a family. Amy was born in San Jose, California, on May 15, 1978. Her brother, Kevin, was born in 1979. From the start, the Chows were determined that their children would have the best of what America had to offer. Although Mr. and Mrs. Chow continued to speak their native language to each other, they insisted that Amy and Kevin learn English as their primary language. "My parents didn't want me to have an accent," Amy explains. "And I had an American baby-sitter. But now I would like to learn the Chinese language and Chinese history."

Two-year-old Amy loved to give her baby brother, Kevin, lots of hugs.

At home, the Chows embraced American culture while holding on to traditions in cooking and decorative arts. One of Amy's favorite things is a painting of fish that her grandmother created in a traditional Chinese style. Amy also prefers her mother's Chinese cooking to most American foods. "I like her broccoli beef," Amy says with a smile. "But I can eat just about anything—my very favorite food is spaghetti."

When Amy was three years old, Mrs. Chow wanted to enroll her in ballet classes. She herself had once had dreams of being a ballerina. But the local ballet school said Amy was too young. After looking around, Mrs. Chow found the West Valley Gymnastics School in Campbell, California, which had a tot gymnastics class. Amy has now been there for fifteen years.

Like Amanda Borden, Amy started with weekly lessons but soon switched to a more demanding schedule because of her obvious innate talent. When Amy was six, Mary Lou Retton burst on the scene and stole everyone's heart at the 1984 Olympics. "I wanted to be like Mary Lou," Amy recalls. "I sensed she was enthusiastic and happy. I idolized her." After Mary Lou won the gold medal in Los Angeles, the idea of someday aiming for the Olympics occupied the back of Amy's mind.

Courtesy of Chow family

Dressed as Wonder Woman, Amy headed out with Superman Kevin for a jack-o'-lantern-filled Halloween (1982).

Amy's younger brother, Kevin, is also a gymnast. He hopes to qualify for the Olympics in the future. "In men's gymnastics, their development is later than in women's," Amy explains. Having a sibling who's a gymnast is a big help to her. "I can talk to my brother about skills I'm having problems with," she says. "He knows the language."

For Amy, the years of training have been smoother than for some of her fellow teammates. She has stayed with the same gym and the same two coaches, Mark Young and Diane Amos, since she was three years old. "They're both so understanding and supportive of me," she says. Young teaches Amy tumbling, the vault, and the uneven parallel bars. "I spend more time with him than I do at home," Amy says. "Mark is like a second father to me. He understands me, and he isn't pushy." Diane Amos works with Amy on the balance beam and the floor exercise, which Amy finds her biggest challenge.

Amy was always eager to practice on the balance beam in her California backyard (1986).

Not wanting to be a show-off, Amy had to learn to strut her stuff. "Diane would tell me to express myself and lift my head higher," she remembers. "That was the hardest thing for me to do." Along with Diane Amos, choreographer Geza Pozsar helped Amy choose her floor exercise music and develop her routine.

Amy and her brother, Kevin, had a great time when they went fishing with their cousin in 1983.

Courtesy of Chow family

Amy always looked forward to going to West Valley Gymnastics School in California (1987).

Amy's favorite event is the uneven parallel bars, because she can develop original skills like the Chow one and Chow two (two Stalder twisting moves named after Amy) for the apparatus. It's no wonder she won the silver medal for it!

Amy has had her share of sprained ankles—including one that caused her to miss the 1995 World Championships—but no broken bones or more serious injuries. "Every injury is a setback," she says, "but you have to say to yourself, 'I want to do this, I'll stick with it, and I'll come back.'" She remembers one low point when she briefly questioned whether it was all worth it. "It lasted a short time. Everyone has those moments. But once I got back to the gym, I knew this was what I wanted to do. When I started it, I loved it, and I knew I would stick with it. I've devoted my life to gymnastics because I want to—I do it for myself." She enjoys practicing and competing but says, "Applause is not the reason I love gymnastics. I don't like to be a show-off. I just enjoy doing this. Competing is part of the process. I've realized it takes a lot of hard work, commitment, and maturity. But it has to be fun, also. Once it stops being fun, it's probably not worth it."

Perhaps Amy handles the stresses and intense pressure of gymnastics so well because she makes time for a diverse range of interests. Her parents offered her many different opportunities as she was growing up. "My mom and dad would let me try different things to see if I liked them," she says. "I'm not nervous when I try new things. That's what makes it fun."

For years Amy dived competitively, focusing on springboard diving, which came naturally to her. "When I started competing in gymnastics in the summer, about

Amy is an accomplished pianist. In 1996 she played a recital in a San Jose retirement home.

four years ago, I had to give up competitive diving," she explains. "Diving was fun, but gymnastics is even better. It's extremely challenging, and it's taught me to be efficient."

Her main method of relaxation these days is playing classical music on the piano. A piano student since the age of five, she is considered very gifted. "The piano gives me time to myself," she explains. "I can relax and unwind at the piano." She prefers Bach concertos and Haydn sonatas to any popular music. And just as in gymnastics, where she prefers performing to watching, Amy would rather play music herself than listen to recordings.

THE MAGNIFICENT SEVEN

Courtesy of Chow family

At the 1994 U.S. Championships in Nashville, sixteen-year-old Amy showed her beautiful moves on the beam.

While her busy schedule keeps Amy from doing some things, she has never felt that she sacrificed anything she wanted to do in her quest to become an Olympian. "If I want to read a book, I make the time," she says. It's also very important to her that her friends treat her "like a normal person." She says, "I'm very shy until I get to know someone better. Once I feel comfortable with someone, I usually talk more, joke around, and do more things with them." She has both gymnast and nongymnast friends. "My school friends are very excited for me!" Like any other teenager, she enjoys going to the movies, swimming, and just hanging out.

Amy and her brother, Kevin, share a close bond (1996).

In June 1996 Amy graduated from Castilleja High School with honors and a grade-point average above 4.0. Once she had finished with school, her coaches intensified her training schedule in preparation for the Olympic Trials. Amy would spend almost the whole day in the gym, training from about nine-thirty in the morning until twelve-thirty, then taking a break and working out again from about four o'clock until about seven-thirty.

THE MAGNIFICENT SEVEN

Duomo/Ben Van Hook

Amy shows agility on the uneven parallel bars at the 1996 Olympics.

The Olympic Trials in Boston might have put more pressure on another competitor, but not Amy. With her coaches' support, she went to the trials determined to do her best and to find a place on the women's gymnastics team. While she was performing on the beam, usually one of her strongest events, she slipped, scraping her face as she fell to the ground. Despite a wide scratch and a black eye that lasted almost three weeks, she turned in scores impressive enough to ensure her inclusion in Team USA.

Ed Reinke/AP

Amy fiercely concentrated as she approached the vault during the 1996 Olympics.

She was thrilled to qualify for the team and looked forward to getting to know her teammates better. Along with Amanda Borden, Dominique Dawes, Shannon Miller, Dominique Moceanu, Jaycie Phelps, and Kerri Strug, Amy settled into a large fraternity house on Atlanta's Emory University campus. It was a mixed blessing in some ways, Amy recalls. Because they weren't in the Olympic Village, they sometimes felt cut off from the other athletes. But it also offered the opportunity to live close together for the seventeen days of the Olympics, giving the seven young women a chance to feel like sisters, which Amy enjoyed. "We were like a big family living in a pretty house. We knew each other from meets and trials before the Olympics," she explains, but living together and then winning the gold turned the Magnificent Seven into a family.

THE MAGNIFICENT SEVEN

On the uneven bars at the 1996 Olympics.

The night of the optionals, Amy surprised herself by feeling "not as nervous as I thought I'd be. I was prepared. We had all put time, energy, and concentration into our routines. We were there to do them."

Was she distracted by the roaring support of the Atlanta home crowd? "No," she says. "I wasn't even aware of the crowd when I did my routine. When you focus on your routine, you're inside your own head. You automatically do what you've done a million times over." Later, however, she was cheered by the unconditional goodwill of the audience. "The crowd really supported us," she remembers. "They were screaming, and flashbulbs were popping all over the place."

The Magnificent Seven now has plans for a thirty-city tour, which should run until at least mid-November. Although Amy is excited about seeing many new cities, she is disappointed that she must put off starting premed courses at Stanford University. "I kind of wish I could be starting now," she says. "I'm planning on a career as a pediatrician. But the tour is something I didn't expect and really don't want to miss." Once the tour is over, she plans to take courses at a junior college so that she will be up to speed when she does enter Stanford.

Amy got advice from her coach Mark Young during the 1996 Olympics.

In July 1996 the U.S. women's gymnastics team made history, thanks in part to one athlete who was making history on her own—by winning a silver medal on the uneven bars and by being the first Asian American on Team USA. Amy Chow is an American champion many times over.

© Dave Black 1996

Amy likes to invent new moves on the uneven parallel bars (1996 Olympics).

THE MAGNIFICENT SEVEN

Duomo/William R. Sallaz.

At the 1996 Olympics, Amy captured an individual silver medal for her beautiful performance on the uneven parallel bars.

Duomo/Seven E. Sutton

Dominique
Dawes

DOMINIQUE DAWES

VITAL STATISTICS

BIRTHDATE: NOVEMBER 20, 1976
HEIGHT AND WEIGHT: 5 FT, 2-1/2 IN, 110 LBS
HOMETOWN: SILVER SPRING/TAKOMA
PARK, MARYLAND
PARENTS: DON AND LORETTA DAWES
SIBLINGS: DANIELLE, 23, AND DON, 13
CLUB: HILL'S GYMNASTICS
COACH: KELLI HILL
BEGAN GYMNASTICS: 1983

"Like at any other meet, I was trying to stay confident," Dominique Dawes *says. "I was telling myself it was like practice, and to just perform. Performance was the main factor in my routines, because if I performed well, then everything else would go smoothly."*

But it wasn't like any other meet. It was the 1996 Atlanta Olympic Games, and Dominique was part of the American women's gymnastics team. With fourteen years of hard work, persistence, injuries, and practice behind her, Dominique had two goals: a team medal and an individual medal. She achieved both.

Dominique (left) had fun at her cousin Monica's birthday party.

"The team gold medal means a lot. I wanted to do it first for my country and then for the team," she says. "But I'm glad I stayed strong and performed well on the [individual] floor exercise and won the bronze. I was pretty pleased with that performance, but I wish it could have come in on the all-around competition."

After the American team pulled into second place during the compulsories, the pressure was on to perform even better during the optionals. The seven athletes had to pull together and stay focused. "The team was great," Dominique says. "We were all rooting for each other. That was the spark plug in our win. For about three weeks before the Olympics, we had to train together and eat together and live together, and that really helped us."

During the 1992 Olympics the women's team had been housed in the Olympic Village in Barcelona, where there were considerable noise and many distractions, but in 1996 Team USA stayed in a fraternity house on the Emory University campus. "It was easier," says Dominique. "So much more peaceful."

Dominique (right) with her older sister, Danielle (center), and her cousin Monica.

Dominique liked the desert setting of the 1988 U.S. Classic in Arizona.

The weeks of team training helped the seven gymnasts form a sisterhood, but when it came down to the wire, each athlete had to perform individually. "I try to treat every competition, even the Olympics, as a practice," says Dominique. "I get nervous before every competition, because I set high expectations for myself. But if I think of it just as a practice, then I can focus on the routine at hand, and not worry about the crowds, or other people's expectations, or the media, and just focus on my performance."

For the optionals, the American team's first event was the uneven parallel bars. "The bars are a strong event for me," Dominique says. "I knew I could do a strong routine. But in the back of my mind I remembered the World Championships, when I ended up trying way too hard and lost control of my swing. So I really needed to calm myself down inside." To the appreciative Georgia Dome audience, Dominique looked calm, cool, and collected. Her bars routine earned a 9.837, one of the highest scores of the night.

At the 1992 World Championships in Paris, Dominique enjoyed strolling along the city streets.

Courtesy of Dawes family

"I felt confident on the beam, because I had done a good bars routine. Kelli [Dominique's coach, Kelli Hill] was on the sidelines, helping me calm myself down. Just her presence, her being there and smiling, allows me to feel comfortable. If she feels comfortable in knowing I can do it, then I trust her, and I know I can do it well."

Dominique's powerful floor exercises have been a trademark through the years. "I was having trouble staying in bounds in practices," she reports. (Gymnasts must not step off the forty-by-forty-foot floor exercise mat during a routine.) "Thank goodness Kelli got a little tough with me and said I had to stay in bounds during practices. That was my main goal during the performance—just staying in bounds and performing to the audience." Another high score, 9.85, that night at the Olympics showed that Dominique had more than met her goal.

"On the vault, I tried to focus on the landing. The kind of vault I do has a blind landing [meaning that the gymnast must land properly without seeing where she is going], and it's more difficult." Dominique scored a 9.762 for her vault, and her score helped to push the American team ahead of the Russians. Minutes later Dominique Moceanu would miss both her vault landings. Then Kerri Strug would rack up the final score with her gutsy second vault.

THE MAGNIFICENT SEVEN

And Dominique Dawes would be part of Olympic history.

"My most thrilling moment," she says, "was pulling together as a team and just working so hard at practicing all day. Then we all stood together on the awards stand, getting our medals. I knew it was all worth it."

But for Dominique, whose consistently high scores had ranked her the sixth best all-around and second in the optional exercise, the Olympic challenge wasn't over yet. Four years earlier, in Barcelona as a fifteen-year-old athlete, she had helped the American women's gymnastics team win the bronze. But she had come home empty-handed in the individual events. During this, her last Olympics, she was determined to change that.

Dominique's little brother, Don, with their father.

She originally qualified for the all-around competition, as well as the vault and bars. Then Kerri Strug, who had qualified for the individual floor exercise and vault, was injured. Dominique Moceanu took her place for the vault, and Dominique Dawes replaced Strug for the floor exercise. Ironically, it was for this floor exercise that Dominique Dawes received the bronze medal.

Is there a difference between team competition and individual competition for Dominique? Not really, she says. "The only difference for me is, if you do your best and help the team win, six other people will be up on the award stand with you. A lot of people think if you're doing it for the team, then you're doing it for everybody else. But for me, whether it's team or individual, I'm always trying to do my best for me. I compete against myself. When I'm doing it for myself, I know I can do really well and set higher expectations."

Dominique started gymnastics at the age of six, when her parents decided it would be better to channel her energy into that activity than to have her constantly leaping from sofa to chair or sliding down stairs. "I had a lot of energy around the house, and my parents wanted me to use it someplace other than on the furniture," Dominique says with a laugh.

Her older sister, Danielle, now twenty-three, was a role model. "My sister was very active," Dominique recalls. "I liked chasing after her, so I became very active too." (Dominique also has a younger brother, Don, who is now thirteen.)

Mr. and Mrs. Dawes enrolled Dominique at the Wheaton Marva Tots and Teens Gym in Wheaton, Maryland, which was close to their hometown, Silver Spring. It was there that Dominique met Kelli Hill, who has now been her coach for fourteen years. Today the club is called Hill's Gymnastics and is headquartered in Gaithersburg, Maryland.

Unlike many gymnasts, Dominique did not idolize any particular Olympic star when she was young. She liked the sport, had fun doing it, but "it was just another activity" until she was further along in her training. She recalls her first

local competition, when she was ten. "It was me and my best friend. We were the only two in our age group. I won every event, and she was second in every event. It was a great experience for us. Looking back on it, it was really funny. We were trying our hardest, but we were falling all over the place. But it was great that we were able to just get back up and keep going."

Her first gymnastic influence appeared soon afterward. "When I was older, maybe eleven, I noticed Daniella Silvas's style. It was 1987, and Daniella was doing really well then. I can't say I idolized her, but I liked her style and saw how she was unique and different from the rest. It had an impact on me."

During the 1994 Team World Championships in Brisbane, Dominique couldn't resist cuddling a koala bear.

THE MAGNIFICENT SEVEN

Dominique and her longtime coach, Kelli Hill.

When she was twelve, Dominique came up with her personal philosophy, which she calls D-3. It stands for Determination, Dedication, and Dynamics. "I created it to psych me up and get me ready." To further inspire herself, she wrote *Determination, Dedication, Dynamics* in large letters on her bathroom mirror. It would serve as a constant reminder to keep going. In the meantime, she supplemented her gymnastics classes with ballet and jazz dance.

"I started ballet even before gymnastics," she points out, "when I was five or so. And then I got really involved in gymnastics." One of the team coaches and choreographers, Donna Craig, played an important part in Dominique's successful development. "We took dance classes two or three times a week. I liked to do jazzy routines, and I always used jazzy, upbeat music. Before the '92 Olympics, dance instructor Toby Townson came to Hill's and worked diligently on my leg and arm lines and all dance moves. This constant instruction improved my dance abilities further. And preparing for the '96 Olympics, dance instructor and coach Linda Johnson did the same as well." Dominique's emphasis on dance, she believes, helps her to appear naturally graceful. "You have to keep up with dance, especially if you don't have the natural lines. I have to keep up with it because otherwise I would be stiff and my movements wouldn't flow. I've been doing it for so long that my body is accustomed to it, and accustomed to certain lines that are expected. That is, most of the time."

Dominique's senior prom is an event she's glad not to have missed. From left: Dominique's mother, Loretta; Dominique's date; her father, Don.

Some gymnasts live at home during their training years, and some live away from their families at their training centers. Dominique did a little bit of both. Until 1991 she lived at home and went to a regular school. But when she and Kelli decided that Dominique would prepare for the 1992 Olympics, her training intensified. The Dawes family lived about forty-five minutes away from the gym, so a six A.M. workout meant getting up at four-thirty. Then one of her parents would have to drive Dominique to Gaithersburg. So Dominique simply moved in with Kelli Hill and her family. "Kelli and her husband, Rick, have two boys, Ryan and Jason. They were really close, and they gave me the support and nurturing I needed, just like my family back home. Kelli's been there for me the whole time, and she's picked me up and kept me motivated."

Dominique also credits her parents with giving her unconditional support. "But they haven't been pushing me, or giving me advice or anything. It's been up to me [to do] the job I want to do." She appreciates the fact that her parents have allowed her to choose her own path.

Although living with the Hills made traveling and training much easier, it wasn't all smooth sailing. "As a family, we [the Daweses] had to sacrifice a lot," Dominique says. "I spent a lot of time at the gym, so that was hard. But we all learned to work around it, and spent time on the weekends together. Living away, we learned to deal with it. We were setting goals, and everyone had to sacrifice a little bit. But the sacrifices were worth it."

Another difficult aspect of the arrangement was that Dominique had to switch schools in the middle of tenth grade. "It was awkward because I went to a new school and didn't really know anybody," she says. "I felt like I

Duomo/Ben Van Hook

Dominique's awesome moves on the uneven parallel bars at the 1996 Olympics made audiences gasp.

wasn't really there. I didn't get to finish the school year—I had to leave early, before the Olympics, to start training with the Olympic team."

The 1992 Olympics in Barcelona were an eye-opening experience for Dominique. At fifteen, she was one of the youngest members of the team. (Kerri Strug, then fourteen, was also a team member, as was Shannon Miller, then fifteen.) The American team won the bronze, but Dominique failed to qualify for any of the individuals. But she wasn't discouraged. She set her sights on the 1993 World Championships in Birmingham, England.

In 1993 Dominique began to come into her own as a gymnast. At the World Championships, she scored fourth in the all-around (against an international field) and received two silvers, for the uneven parallel bars and the balance beam. She topped that performance at the U.S. National Championships in Salt Lake City, where she won gold medals for the vault and the balance beam, silvers for the all-around and the floor exercise, and a bronze for the uneven bars. The world began to sit up and take notice.

But it was in 1994 that Dominique reached one of the pinnacles of her young life. Besides being queen of the senior prom at Gaithersburg High and graduating with honors, she had a stellar year athletically. At the American Cup in Orlando she swept the field, taking the gold in the all-around, the vault, the uneven bars, the balance beam,

© Dave Black 1996

On the beam at the 1996 Olympics.

and the floor exercise. After that incredible showing, she—astoundingly—bettered her performance at the U.S. National Championships in Nashville. For the first time since 1969, one female athlete took home the gold medal in all five individual events: the all-around, the uneven bars, the balance beam, the vault, and the floor exercise. Dominique Dawes was the one to watch, and

"Awesome Dawesome" (as Dominique had been nicknamed by the media in 1992) reigned as the top gymnast.

Then, in 1995, the dream seemed to fall apart. In February Dominique suffered a stress fracture in her foot that forced her to withdraw from a competition. She tried to maintain her conditioning by focusing on the uneven bars (which are relatively easy on the feet), only to pay for it with another stress fracture, in her wrist. This time she wore a cast for two weeks and then a brace for another two weeks.

"It was a difficult year for me because I was constantly injured but in different parts of my body," Dominique says. "After I qualified for the World Championships, I had to choose between performing well at the Olympics in 1996, hopefully pain-free, or competing in the Worlds and possibly having to deal with pain from then until sometime after the Olympics."

By 1996 Dominique was ready to let the world know she was back on top. At the U.S. Nationals, she won gold medals once again for four individual events: the vault, the uneven bars, the balance beam, and the floor exercise. At the same time, she put to rest rumors that, at nineteen, she was too old for her sport. (Shannon Miller and Amanda Borden are also nineteen, and also endured questions about their continuing ability.)

Without looking back, Dominique made the commitment to train for the 1996 Games. Her grueling schedule started at six in the morning and ended at nine. She rested until three, then worked out again until eight in the evening. The hard work was merely a stepping-stone to achieving her goal. "This year I decided I wanted to make something of my life. I wanted people to remember me, so I wanted to give it all I have. I wanted people to remember me for my strong character."

Dominique had met all her Olympic teammates before, at training camps, meets, and competitions. She believes their personal styles and characters made them each unique. "There was not one person on the Olympic team who was anything like another. We were all different." In fact, the diversity of the team made it seem truly American, with representation from different ethnic backgrounds and geographic regions.

Amy Chow was the only Asian American. Dominique Dawes was the only African American. "It definitely makes me feel special," she says. "I think it's great when little kids look up to me and maybe get aspirations of their own. Not necessarily being an Olympian, but setting other goals and doing their best. Too often people set their [hopes] on Olympic gold, but that's out of reach in the beginning. You have to have stepping-stone goals that are within reach. Once you keep getting up those stepping-stones, you'll reach the pinnacle of your goals and your dreams."

For the immediate future, Dominique will concentrate on the gold medal tour with her teammates. She is also planning to compete in professional competitions and do promotions, endorsements, tours, "and other things that come my way." Her long-term goals include finishing her college education. She has been accepted at Stanford University, where she plans to study either criminal justice or acting—she hasn't decided. "I consider gymnastics to have a little bit of acting in it. You have to walk into the arena with a game face, showing complete and utter confidence. A little smile definitely would not hurt. And the floor exercise is a complete performance [for] the audience."

Training for her second Olympics has taught Dominique that, no matter what, she must keep going. That spirit and persistence have brought Awesome Dawesome to the top. That, and her D-3 philosophy.

Tony Duffy/AllSport

Dominique's effortless grace shined throughout her floor exercise performance (1996 Olympics).

THE MAGNIFICENT SEVEN

Duomo/Rick Rickman

At the 1996 Olympics, Dominique won the individual bronze medal for her floor exercise.

SHANNON MILLER

VITAL STATISTICS

BIRTHDATE: MARCH 10, 1977
HEIGHT AND WEIGHT: 5 FT, 97 LBS
HOMETOWN: EDMOND, OKLAHOMA
PARENTS: RON AND CLAUDIA MILLER
SIBLINGS: TESSA, 21, AND TROY, 15
CLUB: DYNAMO GYMNASTICS
COACHES: STEVE NUNNO, PEGGY LIDDICK
BEGAN GYMNASTICS: 1983

"Competing is my favorite part of gymnastics," says Shannon. "I just love being out there. I love the challenge."

On the first day of the women's gymnastics team compulsories, Shannon Miller recalls, she was nervous. "There were so many people I wanted to please. I mean, there you are, and you're alone, representing your state and your country, and you definitely want to please your coaches and your family and make them proud. There are so many people who have invested their time and energy into what you and you alone are doing at that moment. So I was nervous at first. But once I decided I would go out there and give one hundred percent, then I knew everybody would be happy no matter what happened."

43

Courtesy of Miller family

Two-year-old Shannon always liked to tag along with her older sister, Tessa.

After that night of compulsory routines, the American women's team was in second place, behind the Russians. Shannon knew the real test would be the optionals, scheduled for a couple of days later. Traditionally, the Americans had not done well in compulsories, so it was a definite coup to be in second place after the first day of competition. Nevertheless, the optionals would require everything the team had to give. But this year the elusive team gold medal seemed more tantalizingly close than ever before.

Courtesy of Miller family

The Miller children in 1981 (from left): Tessa, Troy, Shannon.

THE MAGNIFICENT SEVEN

For the past four decades, teams from what was then the Soviet Union and from Romania had dominated women's gymnastics: Since 1952, Soviet women had earned the team gold in every Olympics except 1984, when they boycotted the Games. In that year, Romania won. But never before had the Americans made such a strong showing in the compulsories. And never before had an American team been made up of three former or current national champions: Dominique Dawes, Shannon Miller, and Dominique Moceanu. All seven members had performed in at least one World Championship. Dominique Dawes, Kerri Strug, and Shannon Miller were also veterans of the 1992 Barcelona Games. It was a rock-solid team. And the member with the most experience and the most decorations? Shannon Miller.

Courtesy of Miller family

At age five, Shannon was already at home on the balance beam.

The night of the optionals, competitors from four countries were performing simultaneously on different apparatuses on the floor of the Georgia Dome. Music from the other teams' floor exercise routines blared as the Americans worked through their rotations. "We talked about that afterward with Mary Lee Tracy," says Shannon. (Tracy was one of the two head coaches for the team. The other was Marta Karolyi.) "We didn't even realize the other gymnasts were there! We were so caught up and so focused, it was as though we were the only ones on the floor. And we were so excited at the end when the results were known, we could hardly believe there was still a competitor on the beam!"

For the optionals, Team USA started with the uneven parallel bars, then rotated through the balance beam, the floor exercise, and the vault. Shannon agrees with her teammates that the home crowd provided terrific inspiration. "It's great to have that crowd with you the whole way through," she says. "The crowds and the excitement in the air both give you that adrenaline that makes you push and focus extra hard. As we walked from one event to the next and heard 'Go, U.S.A.!' and our names shouted out, it was just incredible!"

But for Shannon, once it's time for the routine, "everything and everyone disappears, and you're up there alone. If you let it distract you, it would," she admits. "But that's part of the discipline and the training. If you even thought of the crowd, it would make you nervous."

At last it was time for the final rotation. "I knew going into the vault that we were way ahead," says Shannon. "When Dominique Moceanu missed her landings, we got a little worried. But I looked up at the scores and I knew it didn't matter. We all stuck together throughout, and that was what it took."

Courtesy of Miller family

Seven-year-old Shannon loved dressing up in her mother's clothes.

That was what it took for the American women to carry home the team gold medal for the first time in Olympic history. To Shannon, the team gold was especially meaningful. "We all realized that we couldn't have gotten the medal without any one person. We all had to get together and help each other out. We all had to hit it the same day and the same time!"

But winning the team gold was only part of Shannon's personal Olympic victory. Later in the week, she became the only American female gymnast to capture an individual gold medal, for the balance beam. "That was really exciting," she says with understatement. "I was happy to be able to hear the national anthem just one more time." Shannon says she knew deep down she possessed the skill to medal but had some temporary doubts. "I really wanted to hit the routine I knew I was capable of, and after I landed my dismount, I felt this was definitely one of my best beam performances. While my score was good, I still had to wait for four more gymnasts to compete. As we came down to the last person and my score was still holding, I was so excited."

After the seven other gymnasts had performed their beam routines, the scoreboard flashed the information that Shannon's score, 9.862, had beaten that of Ukraine's Lilia Podkopayeva by three eighths of a point. And Shannon had the gold! "It was a fantastic note on which to end my Olympic competition," she says.

Courtesy of Miller family

Shannon showed great form on the beam at the 1989 McDonald's American Cup.

Today, looking at Shannon, the most consistently successful, most decorated, most experienced gymnast America has ever known, it's hard to believe that when she was a toddler her legs turned severely in and she had to wear a corrective shoe bar. "Most people don't know that when I was less than a year old, I had to wear this brace around the clock, taking it off only for baths," she says. "The doctor was amazed that I learned to crawl in the brace, and when it was taken off right before my first birthday, I walked a couple of weeks later, right on schedule. My parents were amazed."

Shannon worked hard to keep up with her sister, Tessa (now twenty-one). They both desperately wanted a trampoline for Christmas (a few months before Shannon's fifth birthday). Santa brought one, and both girls taught themselves flips on it in just a few weeks.

Ron and Claudia Miller, Shannon and Tessa's parents, enrolled both girls in a noncompetitive recreational program at a gym in their hometown, Edmond, Oklahoma. The program stressed gymnastics, and Shannon was immediately hooked. "I started out at once or twice a week," she remembers, "but after a few months the coach wanted to move us into a more intense program requiring that we go to the gym four days a week." Tessa was not enthusiastic about this change and decided to take art lessons. Shannon, however, was eager to go as often as possible. Her mother had doubts about how long Shannon's enthusiasm would last, but her father, who had a more flexible summer schedule as a university professor, was willing to drive her to gym class every day. Shannon had always followed in Tessa's footsteps, but she now made it clear she was going to do gymnastics even if Tessa didn't.

Shannon's mother and father are far from stage parents. "My parents have always supported me in my gymnastics," says Shannon. "But they had some doubts about how long I would stick with it when the training hours kept increasing. My dad always said that as long as I wanted to go to the gym he'd keep driving." Luckily, Shannon's father could schedule his classes around the travel times. "He's been great," Shannon says. "He's had to drive me to and from the gym at odd hours for so many years."

Courtesy of Miller family

The Miller family (from left, front row): Troy, Claudia, Ron; (in back) Shannon and Tessa.

THE MAGNIFICENT SEVEN

Shannon and her beloved dog, Dusty (1995).

Courtesy of Miller family

The first turning point in Shannon's gymnastics career came when she was nine years old. She was chosen to travel to Moscow with a group of American gymnasts and coaches to observe the Russian gymnastics training program. "That trip gave me a chance to see the Russians training and having so much fun for all the hard work they put into it," she recalls. "I realized they really enjoyed gymnastics."

The trip was also important because Shannon met Steve Nunno, a coach from Oklahoma who had come to observe the Russians. When Shannon returned to Edmond, she asked her parents to switch her to Dynamo Gymnastics, Nunno's training center in nearby Norman, Oklahoma. She has now been with him for eleven years.

"I know it was frustrating for Steve at first, because I cried a lot," Shannon admits. "If I didn't get a skill as perfect as I wanted it, I cried. He worked with me to help me understand that's not the way to handle it."

Once Shannon started training at Dynamo, her gymnastics skills improved incredibly. Unlike many gymnasts training at her level, Shannon has always been able to live at home with her parents and attend regular schools. "I needed that balance," she says. "I was able to live a normal family life, which was extremely important to me. I did miss out on after-school activities, but I got so much from gymnastics that I don't feel I made any sacrifices. I was able to keep my school friends from home because I'd go to school with them all day."

One strategy that helped Shannon keep her "balance" was that she didn't discuss gymnastics with her school friends. "Basically, I led a double life," she says with a laugh. "At school I'm pretty quiet and keep to myself. I know I really have to get my work done, and I don't have a lot of time to talk and socialize. I'm there to learn and get good grades, and I really try to be organized. I don't have any minutes to waste."

Meanwhile, Shannon was juggling an intensive training and competition schedule that soon had her traveling all over the world. Again and again she competed against older and more experienced gymnasts, and again and again she came away with medals of all colors.

Then came the 1992 Olympics in Barcelona. Shannon, after missing the Nationals, won the Olympic Trials, confirming what her parents already knew. Their daughter was determined to go the distance. Steve Nunno laid plans to get his top gymnast in shape to compete head to head with the reigning gymnast of the time, Kim Zmeskal. Kim had won gold medals at the 1991 and 1992 World Championships and, along with Shannon, would be on the American women's gymnastics team at the Olympics. Shannon was as strong as Kim, and it was time for the world to know it.

At the 1996 Olympics, Shannon displayed total strength on the beam.

THE MAGNIFICENT SEVEN

Shannon's coach Peggy Liddick worked with her on her balance beam routine. "Peggy's a great coach," Shannon says. "She knows her gymnastics. She's very intelligent and is able to relate gymnastics to me and tell me about it in a way that I can understand—the physics of it and how it relates to geometry—and that's one of my specialties. Peggy would always dream up skills and say, 'Let's try it!' We're on the same wavelength."

Steve worked with Shannon on goal setting—both long- and short-term goals. "I've taken his advice to step back and look at the big picture," Shannon says. "I definitely take one day at a time and realize what my goals are one day at a time. I love challenges, and there are always new skills to

Shannon leaped to great heights during her floor exercise at the 1996 Olympics.

learn. If you can't find it in *The Code of Points*—that's the book of skills—you can always make something up. There's always the extra mile to go, and that's what I've always loved."

Then, shortly before the Games, Shannon broke her arm. "I was fifteen," she recalls. "I hit my feet on the bar on my dismount and came down arms first. They had to put a screw in my elbow for the Games." It was the first of a series of injuries that would plague her during the next several years.

Shannon nailed another move during her 1996 Olympic beam performance.

Duomo/Steven E. Sutton

But a screw holding her bones together was not enough to stop Shannon. At Barcelona, she exceeded everyone's expectations and brought home five medals: silvers for the beam and for all-around and bronzes for the uneven parallel bars, the floor exercise, and the team. She won more medals than any other U.S. athlete.

It turned out that the 1992 Olympics were only a warm-up for Shannon. At the 1993 World Championships, she won three gold medals, including the gold for all-around. At the U.S. Olympic Sports Festival in San Antonio, she set or tied seven gymnastics records. At the 1993 American Cup, she swept the events. She concluded the 1993 season by winning the all-around at the U.S. Championships, along with gold medals on the uneven bars and floor, a silver medal on the vault, and a bronze medal on the beam.

Then, suddenly, Shannon was ready to quit. Hectic competition schedules and increasing pressure to stay number one made her feel burned out. She was only sixteen, but in some ways she had already achieved a lifetime's worth of goals. For years, by choice, she had made gymnastics her life. There had always been another gymnastics goal to strive for. But maybe it was time to move on to other challenges outside gymnastics.

Plenty of soul-searching talks with her parents and with Steve Nunno convinced Shannon to stick it out as a gymnast a little while longer. She set new, short-term goals that would help her rediscover the excitement she'd once felt. For a while, she cut back on training hours and let some of her nagging injuries heal.

With new goals, interest, and determination, she captured five medals (two golds and three silvers) at the 1994 Goodwill Games, and another gold for the all-around at the 1995 Pan-American Games, along with gold for the uneven bars and floor, and silver for the vault. She also won the all-around title and won gold on the beam at the 1994 World Championships, becoming the only athlete ever to win two consecutive years. Those successes helped her decide to stay with gymnastics and go into training for the 1996 Olympics.

But the decision, once made, was difficult to stick to. At the 1995 World Championships, Shannon sprained her ankle. Since the ankle was causing significant pain, the decision was made that Shannon would only compete on the bars. However, as it became apparent that the United States was being severely pressed by Russia and could end up out of the medals, Shannon was needed on all four events. All her scores counted toward the team bronze medal. The United States edged Russia by only .016 of a point, with Shannon the top scorer for the U.S. team. Shortly afterward, Shannon strained her forearm and injured her wrist.

At the 1992 Olympics, at age fifteen, Shannon had been four feet, seven inches tall and had weighed seventy-five pounds. Three years later she was almost five feet tall and tipped the scales at about ninety-four pounds. She was still lithe and muscular, but she had to get used to her new size. Today she says that her height and weight give her more power, especially in the floor exercise. But 1995 was a frustrating, difficult time.

© Dave Black 1996

Shannon glided through her uneven parallel bars routine at the 1996 Olympics.

Then came the turning point. The media, hearing that Shannon was aiming for the 1996 Olympics, began to write articles questioning her ability. She would be nineteen years old at the Atlanta Games (the same age as Amanda Borden and Dominique Dawes). That's quite young for most sports—but not for gymnastics. The field is dominated by thirteen-, fourteen-, and fifteen-year-olds. In the old days, a gymnast was considered hot at fourteen and washed up at sixteen. How would Shannon perform?

"When the media started to write that I was too old for the sport, it was then I decided I would show myself and a lot of other people that I wasn't too old, that I could still learn the skills, and that I had what it takes to win," says Shannon defiantly.

In fact, the gymnastics field at the 1996 Games included several veterans who were eighteen years old or older. They performed at least as well as, if not better than, their younger counterparts.

After such stunning earlier successes, many gymnasts would have rested on their laurels and retired gracefully. Not Shannon. She wanted to go out with a bang, capping an unbeatable career with the ultimate achievement: gold medals at the Olympics. And Shannon reached that goal, as she has reached so many others in her life. She holds the honor of being the most decorated American gymnast, male or female, in history. She has earned seven Olympic medals and nine World Championship medals. Not only that, but she has broken the age barrier in a sport that treats its veterans harshly.

Now that the Games are over, Shannon plans to participate in professional competitions. She also looks forward to traveling around the country with her six teammates on their gold medal tour. After that, she and her family plan to go skiing—her first time in ten years. "I'm really looking forward to it," she says. Then it's back to the University of Oklahoma, where she will pursue a major with an emphasis on math and science, possibly in business.

Does she have any interest in a sports career? "No—I could never be a coach," she says frankly. "I'm a participant. I find it hard to sit back and watch. I don't think I could spend time in a gym without doing gymnastics myself. That would be hard for me."

Duomo/Rick Rickman

Shannon was all smiles after winning the individual gold medal for her flawless beam routine at the 1996 Olympics.

And what will she tell young fans during the gold medal tour? "I'd like to tell kids that gymnastics is a great sport, because it helps you with the coordination, strength, and discipline you need for any sport. It teaches you the value of hard work—that it does pay off. I think it also teaches you about goal setting, which is very important. Your goal doesn't have to be to make the Olympics. Only seven girls will be on the team, out of a whole nation of gymnasts. There are other goals to pursue: college scholarships, national and international competitions . . . most important, you have to get an education and prepare yourself for the world."

The world is now waiting for Shannon Miller—whatever new goals she decides to pursue.

Dominique
Moceanu

DOMINIQUE
MOCEANU

VITAL STATISTICS

BIRTHDAY: SEPTEMBER 30, 1981
HEIGHT AND WEIGHT: 4 FT, 6-1/2 IN, 75 LBS
HOMETOWN: HOUSTON, TEXAS
PARENTS: DIMITRY AND CAMELIA MOCEANU
SIBLING: CHRISTINA, 7
CLUB: KAROLYI'S GYMNASTICS
COACHES: BELA AND MARTA KAROLYI
BEGAN GYMNASTICS: 1985

"This is the biggest Games in history, and we did it," says Dominique. "It's really too hard to explain in words."

Fourteen-year-old Dominique Moceanu came away from the 1996 Olympic Games feeling that she had gotten what she wanted: the team gold medal, a first for American women. Not to mention a rose and a kiss bestowed on her by Russian gold medal gymnast Alexei Nemov!

The night of the all-important optionals, Dominique had a good feeling about the events. She felt prepared, and she liked the order in which the team was to perform.

"I knew we'd start off on bars and then go to the beam," she recalls. "That was great because those are the two pressure events. The floor exercise and the vault are more relaxing. I was very excited after I did my bars routine because it was really good. Everyone got very excited, and we said we'd just have to keep our focus and concentrate. I had a lot of confidence for the beam because I'd just done a good bar. Then, after the beam, I felt calm because I had two other events coming up."

Of all her performances, Dominique was most looking forward to the floor exercise. "I was ready to show the crowd a new floor routine. It was very exciting because the crowd really got into it, so I really enjoyed it. The music was 'The Devil Went Down to Georgia,' a song Bela had heard on the radio. It had great fiddles and a fast beat. When I did a good routine, I knew the team was doing well, and I was really happy. We had one more event, and I was ready, because we were up for first place. It really got the adrenaline going. We were so psyched, and then we had our last event, the vault, and we won!"

During the last event, Dominique lost both of her vault landings. No one was more surprised than she. "Of course I was disappointed," she says, "but you have to be positive and look ahead. It was over. There's no looking back."

In part because of her solid earlier routines, Team USA walked away with the gold medal anyway. "Winning the medal was incredible," says Dominique. "It's a great feeling, just unbelievable. Not many people get gold medals, so everybody's real happy. It's really such an amazing feeling that goes down so deep. It took a while for it to click in for all of us. The first few days we'd say, 'Do you know what we did? We made history!' Just think, my name will be in history books, with everyone else's. It's just all full of emotion. It was hard to believe at first. We kept saying, 'I don't believe it!' And my parents were so happy they were crying, because they know these moments. They dreamed of this moment."

Courtesy of Moceanu family

Nine-month-old Dominique was the center of attention at her baptism party.

Dominique told Santa Claus exactly what she wanted for Christmas 1985.

Courtesy of Moceanu family

Even as she prepared to take part in the thirty-city gold medal tour with her six teammates, Dominique recalled the way she had worked to prepare for the Olympics. "I always tried to think of my goals, think of what I've accomplished, think that I'm going to make it. I told myself, 'It's going to be the Olympics soon. You have to make yourself do it.' Motivation must come from yourself."

She also gives credit to her parents. "My parents motivated me a lot. They've been totally supportive about everything. They want the best for me, and they're always doing everything and anything they can. They made all the sacrifices. Without them I never would have been here. They've done everything in the world for me, and it's really great that I have such support from them." Dominique also got a lot of support from outside her family. "Mac and Linda McInvale at Gallery Furniture helped me out tremendously through the years. I'm very thankful to them."

After the recent change in age requirements adopted by the American Gymnastics Association in Atlanta, Dominique, at fourteen, would have been too young to qualify for the Olympic Trials. But she made it under the wire and had "the time of my life" as a member of the first American women's gymnastics team ever to bring home the team gold medal.

And afterward, "It was incredible," she says. "When I got [back to Houston], everyone was waiting for me. My parents brought me home in a limousine, and it was so neat. We stood around talking with friends and fans and signing autographs. It was great!" The first things she saw when she walked into her family's home were the thousands and thousands of fan letters she had received, along with stuffed animals, flowers, and other gifts. "The post office is going nuts," she says, laughing. "I'm so grateful to everyone who has written to me, and I'm grateful to all my friends. They have all been very kind. America really is an incredible place."

Unlike most of her teammates, who began gymnastics at age three, four, or five, Dominique was introduced to the sport at the tender age of six months. Her father, Dimitry, and her mother, Camelia, had both been gymnasts in their native Romania. After emigrating to America, they promised each other that their first child—male or female—would also pursue gymnastics.

Dominique got her first passport at age five and went on a long trip to Europe with her parents. Here she is riding in a gondola in Venice.

When Dominique was six months old, her parents' wishes seemed to be coming true. Her father tested her strength by letting her grip a clothesline strung across the kitchen. Camelia anxiously waited to catch her baby daughter, but Dominique never let go of the line. "My parents say they knew then that I had what it took," says Dominique.

Two and a half years later, Dimitry called Bela Karolyi at his gym in Houston. Dimitry knew Bela's reputation—Bela had coached Nadia Comaneci to perfect scores at the 1972 Olympics. In 1984 Bela was coaching Mary Lou Retton, who would sweep the events at the 1984 Olympics. Besides, Bela was a fellow former Romanian.

But the famous coach just chuckled at

Courtesy of Moceanu family

Dominique and her little sister, Christina, are very close (1991).

Dimitry's request. "Bela told my dad to get in touch with him again if I still showed promise when I turned nine," says Dominique.

Meanwhile, the Moceanus relocated to Highland Park, a suburb of Chicago, where they enrolled Dominique in her first gymnastics class. In 1985 they moved again, to Tampa, and Dominique took classes at LaFleur's Gymnastics. That was when Dominique started to fulfill her potential as a gymnast. Her parents noted her progress proudly and believed that she truly had been born to be a champion.

It wasn't until she was seven that Dominique herself began to take gymnastics seriously. Until then, going to the gym and learning new skills just seemed like fun to her. "It was at my first local competition, when I heard the audience applaud for me," she says, "that I wished I'd done better." She resolved to sharpen her skills.

With single-minded intensity, Dominique devoted herself to learning as many gymnastics skills as possible, as quickly as possible. "It was hard work, but I knew I could do it," she says.

Soon it became obvious that her skills had progressed as far as they could in Florida. Dominique longed to go to Houston to study with Bela Karolyi, but how could she? Her family lived in Tampa—her parents had jobs and lives there. She and her younger sister, Christina (born in 1989), were both in school. It was impossible.

Then one day Dimitry heard Dominique sighing to herself as she watched a gymnastics exhibition. He had already called Bela and reminded him of their earlier talk. With a laugh, Dimitry assured Bela that Dominique was still showing exceptional promise as a gymnast. Bela relented and said that if Dominique really was that good, he would take her on. "I couldn't believe it when I heard my dad say that we were moving to Houston," says Dominique. "It seemed unreal."

The Moceanus—Dimitry, Dominique, and Camelia— spent New Year's Eve 1993 with friends in Beverly Hills.

A month later Dominique walked into Karolyi's gym for the first time. She was completely overwhelmed. At LaFleur's Gymnastics she had been a big fish in a little pond—their star gymnast. At Karolyi's she was one of many gymnasts, and the many included stars Kim Zmeskal, Betty Okino, Kerri Strug, and Svetlana Boguinskaya. Dominique was only ten years old, and suddenly she was training with some of the best gymnasts in the world. It took her a while to find her way. "All of a sudden I wasn't so sure I wanted my wish to come true," she remembers.

Courtesy of Moceanu family

Dominique loved her fourteenth-birthday Rollerblade party.

On one of her first days there, Dominique had to perform her skills for Bela, his wife, Marta, and choreographer Geza Pozsar. "I was very nervous, and I didn't perform well," says Dominique. "Then Bela told me that I executed a lot of skills sloppily, so I had to start my training practically at the beginning, perfecting each stage of each movement."

Bela was a demanding coach. "At first I was a little scared of Bela," Dominique says. "And training with so many of the gymnasts I'd always admired on TV was intimidating. But I was definitely experiencing the best gymnastic training in the world."

Dominique exhibited determination while she performed her routine on the uneven bars at the 1996 Olympics.

Once she felt more comfortable in her new surroundings, Dominique began to make progress. She relaxed and trusted Bela and Marta to know what was best for her. The warmth and friendliness of her world-class teammates helped her find her niche. Only seven months after beginning her training at Karolyi's, she qualified for the Junior Nationals team. At the 1992 U.S. Nationals competition in Columbus, Ohio, she walked away with a gold medal for the balance beam in the junior division. At ten years old, she was the youngest junior qualifier ever, and the youngest gymnast ever to win a gold medal on the balance beam.

Duomo/Steven E. Sutton

Dominique showed great control on the balance beam at the1996 Olympics.

That success was followed by the 1993 U.S. National Championships, in which she finished seventh all-around in the junior division. By 1994 Dominique had cleaned up her techniques and blossomed as a gymnast. Her parents' faith in her abilities was paying off, and Bela could see that Dominique had what it took to go all the way. By putting herself completely in Bela's and Marta's hands, and by giving unstintingly of herself during each workout and practice, Dominique began to mature as an athlete. Soon she could hold her own against the gymnasts who had so awed her. Now they were just her friends. She was happy for their successes but no longer believed that her own goals were out of reach.

"Bela told me that if I really worked hard and pushed myself, I could achieve my biggest dreams," says Dominique. She took that philosophy to heart, and at the U.S. National Championships in 1994 won gold medals for best all-around, the floor exercise, and the vault, and bronze medals for the balance beam and the uneven parallel bars, all in the junior division.

But it was in 1995 that Dominique began to receive worldwide attention. She performed like a juggernaut that year, winning both gold and bronze medals at the Reese's International Gymnastics Cup. At the American Classic she brought home a gold, a silver, and two bronzes. The 1995 VISA Challenge was a great meet for her: She won her first all-around gold medal against an international field and earned two other gold medals, a silver, and two bronzes. Not bad for a thirteen-year-old!

At the U.S. National Championships in 1995, Dominique competed for the first time in the senior division, against more experienced gymnasts such as Amy Chow, Shannon Miller, Jaycie Phelps, and Kerri Strug. Again Dominique won a gold medal for the all-around. A silver for the floor exercise and a bronze for the vault rounded out her achievement. At thirteen, she was the youngest national champion in history. Shannon Miller came in second, and Jaycie Phelps came in third. "It was incredible to be the national champion," says Dominique. "All my hard work in the gym paid off. It was a real high and gave me a lot of confidence."

The 1995 World Team Trials, and then the World Championships in Sabae, Japan, were also great meets for Dominique. Finishing fifth all-around at the World Championships put the Olympic Trials firmly in her grasp. By the end of 1995, she seemed unstoppable.

The balance beam is one of Dominique's favorite events.

But as every athlete knows, an injury can sideline anyone. Until the summer of 1996, Dominique had been lucky: Injuries had never seriously interfered with her intensive training. Like other gymnasts, she had suffered minor strains and sprains, but she had weathered them calmly. Then the unthinkable happened. Right before the Olympic Trials, she felt pain in her leg that she couldn't ignore. An X ray revealed a four-inch stress fracture in her right tibia. "It was so tough," she says. "I had to stop training. The doctors said that if I didn't, the bone could snap completely. But the Olympic Trials were coming up. No one thought I'd be healed in time."

Duomo/Steven E. Sutton

Dominique loved performing for the crowd during her floor exercise at the 1996 Olympics.

Dominique had come so far that the thought of giving up never crossed her mind. Bela Karolyi petitioned the Olympic Committee to accept his star pupil as an Olympic team member based on the average of her scores at the Nationals. Another top gymnast, Shannon Miller, was also injured before the trials and submitted her scores from the Nationals to the committee.

If seven other gymnasts at the Olympic Trials had scored higher than Dominique's average score at the Nationals, Dominique's dream would have been put on hold. As it was, her inclusion in the team was assured mathematically after the first four rotations. (Shannon Miller was included after three rotations.) Dominique's journey to the Olympics was a reality.

Dominique was tremendously excited when her autobiography was published just before the 1996 Olympics.

Today, with her Olympic success behind her, what lies in store for America's youngest gold medal gymnast? Amanda Borden, Dominique Dawes, Shannon Miller, and Kerri Strug will probably retire from amateur competition because of their ages. But Dominique Moceanu is still only fourteen. "Everyone is already saying, 'Get ready for 2000,'" she reports. "I think I'll stay. It will be too hard to leave. This year I'm committed to pro gymnastics and exhibitions and the gold medal tour. At the beginning of January, I'll have a clean start and try again. When everything is finished and settled, we'll see how things work out and how I feel."

Dominique was encouraged to plan on the 2000 Games by sprinter Michael Johnson, whom she met at the Olympics. "He was great," Dominique says. "He gave me his autograph and said, 'Man, you should go for 2000 because you're still so young!' He's a real inspiration to me."

But Dominique feels mixed emotions when she contemplates four more years of competitive training against a new crop of gymnasts who will be younger than she is. "I want to spend more time with my family, and I'm looking forward to going back to my private school, Northland Christian." (Dominique has been taught at home for the past year.) "During the gold medal tour, I'll be going to school three or four days a week and doing the tour on long weekends." Administrators at her school have been very flexible, she says. "That's great, because I really do want to go back to school. I want to go to school dances and activities. If the kids are going to the mall, or to a basketball game, I want to be able to go too. To most kids it sounds boring, but to me it will be new and fun!"

One large consideration for Dominique is the fact that Bela and Marta Karolyi have announced their intentions to retire. Where does that leave Dominique? Her family moved to Houston just so that she could train with Bela. "We'll see," Dominique says philosophically. "I love Bela and Marta. It was very sad when we said good-bye. But they're entitled to retire—they've done enough. You don't understand how much they've accomplished and how hard they've worked. We all won the gold medal with their help. Now they want to enjoy the rest of their lives, because they've done this forever."

Dominique notes that Bela retired once before but came out of retirement specifically to train her. "It's too much to ask him to do it again. You need that excitement and enthusiasm, and he had it for me. Now he needs a break, and he's earned it."

Like many of her teammates, Dominique sees sports medicine as a long-term goal. Whether she goes to the 2000 Games in Sydney remains to be seen. But she is happy with her life right now. "Everything I wanted from the 1996 Olympics, I got," she says. "But now that I've accomplished it, I'll have to think about things, get some ideas. I'm only fourteen. I guess I'll take it as it comes, easily and smoothly. You have to set a goal for yourself."

Right now Dominique's goal is to schedule a long-overdue family vacation. "I don't care where it is, as long as there's a beach. I just want to lie out, relax, and get a tan."

And she deserves it. But the world will be watching for her in the year 2000.

Duomo/Steven E. Sutton

Jaycie
Phelps

JAYCIE
PHELPS

VITAL STATISTICS

BIRTHDATE: SEPTEMBER 26, 1979
HEIGHT AND WEIGHT: 5 FT, 97 LBS
HOMETOWN: GREENFIELD, INDIANA
PARENTS: JACK AND CHERYL PHELPS
SIBLING: DENNIS, 20
CLUB: CINCINNATI GYMNASTICS ACADEMY
COACH: MARY LEE TRACY
BEGAN GYMNASTICS: 1983

"For a while I lost confidence in my ability to do it," says Jaycie. "But now it's back and I love it."

Looking at sixteen-year-old Jaycie Phelps, a gold medal champion and one of the finest gymnasts in the world, it's hard to imagine a Jaycie who didn't believe in herself. But the twelve-year road to Olympic glory was a long and hard one with many ups and downs. On July 23, as she watched the American flag being raised in her honor, Jaycie finally realized, as she says, "No matter what you want, if your heart is in it and you have a dream, stick with it. Anything is possible!"

Looking back on that history-making night, Jaycie remembers her fears. "The uneven parallel bars was my first event. It was the first routine of the night for the U.S., and I was a little nervous because I had the role of starting the team off. When I finished I was just relieved that I had started the team off well.

"Then I was especially nervous when I got up on the beam, because that's the hardest for me. After the beam, I knew I could have done a better routine, but I had to look forward to the floor exercise.

"After the floor exercise I was really pumped up, because I knew it was probably the best floor exercise of my life, and I was very excited. When I looked at the scoreboard after all of our floor routines, I could see we were almost one point ahead of the Russians. And I knew that if we got through the vault [the last American rotation], we'd have it!"

Courtesy of Phelps family

Jaycie (center) and friends Wendy Whitaker and Lacie Ludwig celebrated her fourth birthday.

For someone who had decided to quit gymnastics only three years earlier, being on the first American women's gymnastics team ever to take home the gold was especially rewarding. "It was amazing!" Jaycie says. "I remember saying, 'I can't believe it!' We were all hugging, laughing, and crying. We knew we had what it took to make it, but when it happened, it was a dream come true."

Jaycie's own routines contributed solidly to the team's overall optionals scores through the four rotations of uneven parallel bars, balance beam, floor exercise, and vault. "Competing as a team definitely helped all of us," Jaycie says. "We were all pushing for each other. It's a lot of fun to be a member of a team, and everyone tried her best. If each member does her best, the team is going to do well and everyone will benefit together. A team wins because of a team effort."

But when the gold medal is on the line, each individual effort counts. "The crowd gave us the extra edge," Jaycie says. "All those cheering fans were helpful on the floor and vault, but I couldn't have that distraction on the beam or the bars. If I allowed myself to hear it, I would get too pumped up, and on the beam and bars I need to be calm. So I blocked out the crowd and all the noise and just focused on my routine."

Once all the scores were in and the members of Team USA knew they had won the gold, Jaycie finally believed she wasn't dreaming. Later that night, the team celebrated at Planet Hollywood. Jaycie recalls, "They had an enormous screen, and they were playing all of our routines. I was nervous just watching it, even though I knew the outcome. We were cheering for each other. We were a team."

Jaycie's talent for gymnastics was discovered almost by accident when she was four years old. One day her nursery-school class in Greenfield, Indiana, went on a field trip to a nearby gym. Jaycie was chosen to demonstrate what the coaches taught at the gym.

"One coach thought I was talented," she remembers. The gym, run by Byron and Teresa Holden, was only ten minutes away from Jaycie's home. Jack and Cheryl Phelps (Jaycie's name is a combination of their first initials) decided to enroll their daughter for lessons. At her young age, gymnastics came easily. Cartwheels? Back flips? No problem. Jaycie felt no fear—ever. Everything came easily to her, effortlessly.

"I just loved it when I was four, and I kept doing it," she says. "I started out with classes once a week, then twice a week, and it kept building."

Jaycie was already taking ballet at age three.

Courtesy of Phelps family

At age five, Jaycie had fun practicing her splits at her grandmother's house.

Eight years later, in 1991, the Phelpses were faced with a tough decision. Jaycie had progressed as far as she could go in Greenfield. To develop her talent further, she would have to find coaches who were more advanced. After a great deal of soul-searching, Jaycie's parents decided to relocate the family to Scottsdale, Arizona, so that Jaycie could study at the Desert Devils Gym there.

The relocation proved extremely difficult for everyone. At first only Jaycie, Mrs. Phelps, and Jaycie's older brother, Dennis, moved out. Mr. Phelps followed later, in 1992. Jaycie missed her father, and it was hard for the family to be split up. Jaycie also missed the extended Phelps family back in Greenfield—her grandparents, cousins, aunts, and uncles. Even after Jack Phelps joined his family the following year, it was still a trying situation. Jack and Cheryl had uprooted their careers, and the family felt as if it were in limbo.

What was worse, Jaycie was not progressing at her gym. In fact, she was regressing. At Jaycie's level of intensive training, the coach-gymnast relationship is exceedingly important. If there is a personality conflict, a basic lack of understanding, it can be disastrous. At Desert Devils, Jaycie wasn't finding what she needed.

THE MAGNIFICENT SEVEN

By 1993 she was ready to quit for good. Her self-esteem was at an all-time low, her skills had stagnated, and, most important, she had lost her love of the sport. At the 1993 Junior USA Championships, she ranked a disappointing twenty-fourth. She looked for excuses not to go back into the gym.

It was her parents, Jack and Cheryl, who convinced her she was too talented to give up. Certain that there was a coach somewhere who would appreciate their daughter's unique abilities, Jack and Cheryl found Mary Lee Tracy at Cincinnati Gymnastics Academy. So the Phelpses moved back to Greenfield, and Jack Phelps resumed his job at the pharmaceuticals company Eli Lilly.

For her first two months in Cincinnati, while Mrs. Phelps was getting organized back in Greenfield, Jaycie lived with the Lichey family. Their two daughters, Karin and Kristi, also studied with Mary Lee Tracy. Although at the time Jaycie was homesick and missed her family, she has remained close to the Licheys and appreciates all they did for her. "I would like to thank them for everything they did while I was living with them," she says. "They were the best family, real friends. They were so supportive of me."

Courtesy of Phelps family

Jaycie displayed great form in her early days of training at age nine.

At first Jaycie continued to feel unsure about gymnastics. Then her mother came to Cincinnati and found an apartment for her and Jaycie to share, and after that things started falling into place. Although the family was split up once again, it was a completely different experience. Mr. Phelps and Dennis were only an hour and a half away in Greenfield, and the family reunited every weekend. "I think the way we lived as a family made us stronger," Jaycie says. "Whenever we had time together, we made it count. We don't take each other for granted."

Once her mother had settled in Cincinnati, Jaycie's life began to turn around. Mary Lee Tracy focused on building Jaycie's self-esteem and provided a warm, nurturing environment that supported the young gymnast while enhancing and developing her technical skills, which were very shaky. Mary Lee also shared her religious faith with Jaycie, and Jaycie responded, feeling that a strong belief in a higher power helped her to rely on herself.

Courtesy of Phelps family

On a trip home to Indiana, Jaycie played with her dog, Bailey (1992).

Between the no-nonsense technical coaching and the strong positive reinforcement that Mary Lee offered, Jaycie finally began to realize the potential she had first demonstrated at the age of four. After she competed in the 1994 Team World Championships in Dortmund, Germany, Jaycie's ranking went from twenty-fourth in the

Jaycie and teammate Amanda Borden shared their joy at making the 1994 World Team with coaches Steve Elliott and Mary Lee Tracy.

junior division to fifteenth in the world in the senior division. Not bad for one year's work, by a gymnast who had been ready to quit!

When Jaycie first started at Cincinnati Gymnastics Academy, she was still attending a local junior high school. "I was in eighth grade, and we had morning and afternoon workouts at school. We started at six-fifteen, while it was still dark, and went till eight-fifteen. After school let out at two-thirty, we worked from three-thirty to about seven-thirty at night." Jaycie's skills thrived under that tough schedule.

For her sophomore year of high school, Jaycie, her parents, and her coach decided to try home schooling. "I went to tutors once a week," Jaycie explains. "They checked my work and gave me assignments for the next week. So I learned to pace myself to get the work done. It helped me become more organized and taught me time management skills that every gymnast needs. It also taught me to be more responsible," she admits. "There are a lot of responsibilities in gymnastics."

Once her home schooling routine had been established, Jaycie spent most of her days in the gym, making up for lost time. From seven in the morning till noon she practiced her skills, learning new vaults and tumbles. Between noon and three she had lunch at home and rested; then it was back to the gym for a workout that lasted from three to about seven in the evening. "It was tough, and pretty much a full day," Jaycie says. But it's the kind of schedule required of a young gymnast with Olympic-size hopes.

"I never thought of myself as having Olympic capabilities until I came to Mary Lee's gym," Jaycie says. "She's a coach who cares about your skills and cares about you as a person. I wouldn't have a gold medal today without Mary Lee."

One thing Mary Lee worked on was Jaycie's readiness for competition. "When I was little, I always tried to, well, show off a little," Jaycie says with a smile. "Because I liked doing gymnastics and it felt good." But that self-confidence was sorely lacking by the time Jaycie switched to Cincinnati Gymnastics Academy. Mary Lee encouraged Jaycie to face the pressure head-on.

"We would put ourselves in meet situations," Jaycie explains. "While we were training, Mary Lee would have the whole gym stop and watch us do our routines. So we felt as if there was a crowd watching us, and it put more pressure on us. We would also use visualization techniques. For example, we would picture an arena in our minds and see ourselves saluting the judges before a routine. Then we would imagine ourselves performing the routine perfectly. We would imagine our perfect scores and see ourselves coming off the award stands, having done our very best."

The results of her hard work showed up in her continuing upward movement in national and world rankings. Then disaster struck. In 1995, three weeks before the World Championships, Jaycie severely injured her left knee, requiring

Courtesy of Phelps family

At the 1995 World Team competition in Sabae, Japan, Jaycie and her mother wore traditional Japanese kimonos to a tea ceremony.

arthroscopic surgery. The old Jaycie would have quit. But the new Jaycie was determined to compete.

Three weeks after surgery, she was back out on the floor in competition. "I competed in only three events, instead of four. I wasn't completely ready for four. It was extremely painful," she admits, "but it was a key competition and I was determined to help the team. It's harder and more painful when you're training after an injury. But when you're actually competing, you get an inner strength, and you focus on the routines and get beyond the pain." That determination helped her team seize third place in the World Championships in Sabae, Japan.

Then it was time to focus on the upcoming Olympic Trials.

For Jaycie, it was very much business as usual, with the added bonus of having her favorite teammate, Amanda Borden, training with her. "We've been working and training together for three years now," Jaycie says. "She's a great friend, and a great teammate. She's like a big sister to me."

As for Olympic training, "It's pretty much just practicing everything over and over until you feel confident with a routine," Jaycie says. Her favorite events are the balance beam and the uneven bars. "I love the beam because it's the most challenging. And the bars? Well, it's just a great feeling. You feel like you're swinging. It's great."

On the beam at the 1996 Olympics.

Like the rest of the Olympic team, she worked with choreographer Geza Pozsar to develop her floor exercise routine. "It's great fun to be in front of a crowd again," she says. "For a while I lost confidence in my ability to do it. But now it's back, and I love it."

There have been many struggles in Jaycie's gymnastics career, many setbacks and hard times. Has it been worth it? "I've had to give up some things," Jaycie says. "But I never really considered them sacrifices. Look what I got out of it: My dream came true!" When she thinks about it, she guesses it would be fun to go to football games and participate in other school activities. "But you can't compare it to traveling around the world, meeting gymnasts from different countries and making new friends. The hardest part has been the language barrier, but sometimes you can be friends as gymnasts because you share that language."

So far Jaycie has been to Germany, Japan, and Puerto Rico. "My favorite was Puerto Rico," she says. "Because of the beach! We had time to just lie around. It was so amazing."

Jaycie performed a beautiful beam routine at the 1996 Olympics.

Jaycie showed control during the beam event at the 1996 Olympics.

With the Games over, Jaycie is looking forward to taking a five-day "girls' vacation" to the Cayman Islands along with her mother; Mary Lee Tracy and her daughter; Jaycie's teammate Amanda Borden; and her best friend, Kristi Lichey. Then there is the thirty-city Olympic gold medal tour she's taking with her teammates. After that, all the Phelpses plan to go on a real family vacation—their first in years.

While not at the gym, Jaycie spends time with her nongymnast friends. "They've been really supportive of what I do, and they don't treat me differently than anyone else. None of them has acted jealous. If anything, they're happy for me and proud of me. It's great to be with them, too, because when you're around the same gymnastic friends twenty-four hours a day, it can be trying."

Duomo/Steven E. Sutton

Jaycie dazzled the crowd during her floor exercise at the 1996 Olympics.

Jaycie's brother, Dennis, is included among her nongymnast friends. A student at Indiana University/Purdue University/Indianapolis (IUPUI), "Dennis has never been jealous of me or wanted to go into gymnastics," Jaycie reports. "He went to a gym once and decided it wasn't for him."

Jaycie is looking forward to her junior year at Northwest High School this fall, even though she will miss some days of the first semester because of the Olympic tour. "I'm glad to be back full days for the first time in what seems like forever," she says. And while on tour, she will have a tutor. In the past her favorite subject was biology, and she is looking forward to a medical career, "perhaps in sports therapy, so I could be with a team." She doesn't see coaching in her future. "When I get finished with gymnastics, I'll be ready for something else," she predicts.

Asked about the 2000 Olympic Games in Sydney, she answers, "That's four years away. It's a long time, and I'm not sure how I'll feel about it. It's always possible, and it's not out of the question, but right now I'm not sure."

During the Olympic tour, which will run until mid-November, many girls are sure to ask Jaycie for advice about becoming gymnasts. "I'll tell them that we enjoy what we do," she says. "To us, it's something fun, not something anyone pressures us to do, or forces us to do, even though it's a lot of work. If you want to be a gymnast, you really have to want to be one. And you have to love it, or it won't be fun."

Jaycie Phelps's career, and her story, are not over yet. How they will end remains to be seen. But whatever her decision about the Sydney Games in 2000, she is, and always will be, an American gold medal champion whose faith and effort made her personal dream come true.

Courtesy of Phelps family

After the team competition at the 1996 Olympics, Jaycie shared her "golden moment" with her parents and her brother, Dennis.

Duomo/Steven E. Sutton

Kerri
Strug

KERRI
STRUG

VITAL STATISTICS

BIRTHDATE: NOVEMBER 19, 1977
HEIGHT AND WEIGHT: 4 FT, 9 IN, 87 LBS
HOMETOWN: TUCSON, ARIZONA
PARENTS: BURT AND MELANIE STRUG
SIBLINGS: LISA, 27, AND KEVIN, 23
CLUB: KAROLYI'S GYMNASTICS
COACHES: BELA AND MARTA KAROLYI
BEGAN GYMNASTICS: 1982

"I had mixed emotions," says Kerri. "I was so ecstatic that we won the gold, but at the same time it was hard because my injury prevented me from achieving my personal goal of competing in the all-arounds and individuals."

The image of eighteen-year-old Kerri Strug's face, contorted with pain after her history-making second vault, will be burned into everyone's mind for years to come. It was the night of the women's gymnastics team optionals, and Dominique Moceanu, a crowd favorite, had just lost both of her vault landings. Until that point, the American team had been solidly ahead. Suddenly it looked as though the gold medal was up for grabs again.

Courtesy of Strug family

The Strug family in 1987 (from left): Kevin, Lisa, Melanie, Burt, and Kerri.

Kerri Strug was the last member of Team USA to vault. Dominique Moceanu had sat down on both of her vaults. Kerri then sat down on her first vault. The crowd in the Georgia Dome went absolutely silent. "At first I couldn't believe it," Kerri remembers. "You train a lot. I didn't expect that to happen, and when I got up, I realized I was hurt. I looked over at Bela and Marta [Bela was Kerri's personal coach; Marta was one of the two head coaches for the team, along with Mary Lee Tracy] and said, 'Something's happened to my foot.' They told me to 'Shake it off, it isn't a big problem,' because they didn't want me to lose my concentration by thinking too much about my leg. I still needed a good vault. They told me, 'Toughen up, you can do it,' because there wasn't a lot of time." Kerri had thirty seconds to perform her next vault, or her first score would count. "I asked Bela what I had to do, and he said nine point six," says Kerri. "I'm eighteen years old—it was my decision."

So she limped back to the starting vault position. "I kept thinking the pain was going to go away," she says. "I kept trying to shake it out, but the pain stayed. I said a quick prayer: 'Please help me out, here!' And then it was time to go. I had to block out the pain and concentrate on hitting my vault."

The emotions of the moment pumped through Kerri. "There was a rush from the adrenaline," she recalls. "The Russians were on the floor exercises, and the vault moves faster. We didn't know how high they were going to score. Vaulting wasn't our strongest event, and our score was a tiny bit low to begin with. I didn't know exactly where we were standing."

Kerri made her decision and saluted the judges. Then she ran at top speed down the runway, without a limp or an off stride. She performed her vault and stuck a perfect landing, both feet solidly on the ground. She saluted the judges again as the thirty-two thousand spectators went wild. Then she collapsed in pain as medics and her coaches ran to her. "I couldn't move. I couldn't walk."

As she was being put onto a stretcher and taken to the medical room, she learned that the American women had won the team gold medal for the first time

Kerri placed first in the floor exercise at the 1989 American Classic meet in Dallas.

Courtesy of Strug family

Kerri celebrated her twelfth birthday at a party with friends.

in the history of the Olympics. One of Kerri's dreams had come true. "Since I was a little girl, watching Mary Lou Retton win the all-arounds, I wanted to be like her. And then there we were: Olympic champions. You can't get much better than that. It was a wonderful feeling."

In the medical room at the Georgia Dome, doctors encased her hurt ankle in a soft cast. "They had called an ambulance to take me to a hospital. Then Bela and Kathy Kelly and my parents came in, and they said I should be able to go to the awards ceremony if I wanted. Of course I wanted to! I had helped the team, and it would be a moment I would never forget. They tried to decide how to get me up there. It had to happen really quick, because I was the last competitor."

Her teammates were lining up for the medals when Strug arrived in a wheelchair. "I told Bela, 'The officials don't want me to go out there,' and he said, 'The New York Police Department couldn't stop me from taking you out there!'"

Then the six-foot, two-inch coach swept up the four-foot, nine-inch gymnast and carried her to the podium. For a second, Kerri felt a little embarrassed because she was still in her leotard and was the only one without her team sweatpants on. But in a moment that feeling was forgotten. "The crowd was so supportive that once I got out there it was all right. It made it more special that Bela was able to come out there. Under normal circumstances he wouldn't have been able to. And he's helped me through so much, I'm glad he could do that for me too."

The moments when Kerri stood on one foot on the podium, next to her teammates, were moments to be cherished. "I think I had more emotional feelings that night than ever before," she admits. "I never imagined that this would take place: that I'd be injured the same night we got the gold. There's no preparation for anything like it."

Kerri, like the other gymnasts, has never feared injuries. "You can't think like that," she says. "We're so well prepared, and we've done these things for years and years. I'm always more worried about how well I'm going to hit it rather than am I going to mess up, or am I going to hurt myself. You should never let those negative thoughts go through your head."

Born in Tucson on November 19, 1977, Kerri was the baby of the Strug family. Her brother, Kevin, was five when she was born, and her sister, Lisa, was nine. Kerri admits that her parents spoiled her because she was the youngest. Both of her siblings studied gymnastics—in fact, Lisa trained at Karolyi's for a while. Kerri followed in their footsteps but notes that for them, "it was more recreational."

Kerri enjoyed a dinner out with her brother, Kevin, and her sister, Lisa (1992).

Her own gymnastics classes began when she was three years old because she wanted to do what Lisa was doing. "If she liked a certain food, then I liked it," says Kerri. "If she wore certain clothes, I wanted to wear them."

In Tucson, Kerri lived at home, attending a small private school and taking after-school gymnastics classes with University of Arizona coach Jim Gault. Her mother, Melanie, sometimes stayed to watch her classes, but not often. "She was never really a gym mom," Kerri reports. "You know, the ones who sit and watch what you do every day. It doesn't help when the parents are there because it's added pressure."

When Kerri was thirteen, she faced a turning point. Judges and coaches were telling her she had major potential. To continue her training, but at an Olympic level, she would have to find another coach. On her own, Kerri decided that she needed to move to Houston and train with Bela Karolyi. "My sister had gone to Karolyi's summer camp. She competed at the Junior Olympics level and did very well," Kerri says proudly.

Nevertheless, Melanie and Burt Strug were upset about Kerri's decision. It would mean breaking up the family; Kerri would room with a family in Houston while the rest of the Strugs stayed in Tucson. And Kerri's brother was just entering college. Suddenly the Strugs' nest was empty.

Courtesy of Strug family

"It was hard on me, because I'm the youngest child, and I'm really close to my parents," Kerri says. "But they visited me a lot. And I knew if I wanted to do this, I would have to make sacrifices." For two years Kerri lived with a family during the week and visited every weekend with her aunt and uncle about an hour and a half from Houston. Her parents would spend holidays in Houston,

Kerri and her parents had a great time on a 1992 family vacation in San Diego.

THE MAGNIFICENT SEVEN

On the beam at the 1996 Olympics, Kerri showed off a strength move.

and the family would gather wherever Kerri was competing. "We're very close, and they're all very supportive," Kerri says.

But her training took its toll. Kerri points out that her gold medal represents "a lot of crying phone calls. My parents had to lift me up. It's hard when you're young. And I'm a little bit rash, and sometimes I'd take things out of perspective and get overly upset."

Training at Karolyi's Gymnastics was often difficult. Acknowledging Kerri's innate sensitivity, Bela tried to treat her a bit more gently than his other gymnasts, whom he expected to be tougher. (After Kerri's incredibly self-sacrificing second vault, Bela professed himself astounded at her courage. "I had not seen this previously in her," he said.)

Kerri was progressing wonderfully and put in solid performances at competition after competition. However, this was during the reign of Kim Zmeskal, Betty Okino, Svetlana Boguinskaya, and a little fireball named Dominique Moceanu, and Kerri was often overshadowed.

In 1992 her solid competitive form qualified her for the Olympic team. Along with Wendy Bruce, Dominique Dawes, Shannon Miller, Betty Okino, Kim Zmeskal, and Michelle Campi, Kerri headed to Barcelona—at fourteen the youngest member of the women's gymnastics team. Her consistently good scores helped Team USA win the bronze, but everyone remembers Shannon Miller's five medals as the highlight of the Games.

In 1993 a severe injury forced Kerri to reevaluate her life's goals. A torn stomach muscle sent her home to Tucson for six months. "I'd already been on an Olympic team," she says, "and I wasn't sure at that point if I wanted

Kerri displayed poise on the beam at the 1996 Olympics.

to just be a normal teenager or go for more. After I was out for a time, I realized I missed gymnastics." In Tucson she had physical therapy and went back to her regular school. Gradually she resumed training.

After getting back into gymnastics in Tucson, "I started conditioning four or five days a week," she remembers. "It took about two or three months to get everything back. It was hard to be out, because I missed key competitions, and my competitors were all doing well. It was hard, but at the same time it was good for me, because I got hungry. Hungry to compete."

By 1995 this dark horse had started to look like a front runner, although she never captured as much press attention as some of her fellow gymnasts. At the U.S. Olympic Festival in Boulder, Colorado, Kerri won golds for the first all-around and the uneven parallel bars, and tied for a bronze on the beam. It was one of her best meets ever, and she began to consider the 1996 Olympics.

For her pre-Olympic training, Kerri moved to Bela's ranch outside Houston, along with Dominique Moceanu. "It was pretty intense, but I knew I wanted the chance to be in the Olympics twice. That was my goal. I knew highly intense training would prepare me the best. We trained from seven-thirty in the morning to about eleven-thirty, and then again from four in the afternoon to seven-thirty at night."

Her hard work paid off: She qualified at the Olympic Trials. She would be part of the American women's team, and she would bring to it her unique qualities.

Besides the excitement of qualifying for the team, Kerri had personal goals of qualifying for individual Olympic events. Her favorite event is the floor exercise,

© Dave Black 1996

Kerri performed a strong beam routine at the 1996 Olympics.

because she believes she's strongest at it. Gymnasts qualified for the individual events based on their scores during the team compulsories. (After the 1996 Games, the team compulsories will be discontinued.) Once Team USA's compulsory round had been completed, Kerri learned she was eligible for the all-around, the floor exercise, and the vault.

But after the crushing blow of a badly sprained ankle, she had to let those goals go. For a few days after winning the gold, she had physical therapy and worked on her routines as best she could, still hoping to compete. But there was no way her ankle would hold up. It was a bitter disappointment. (Dominique Moceanu took her place on the vault and Dominique

America will remember Kerri for her courage at the 1996 Olympics.

Dawes on the floor.) At age eighteen, a two-time veteran of the Olympics, Kerri knew she had lost her final chance.

The gold medal tour awaits Kerri, along with her teammates, but she still has firm plans to enter the University of California at Los Angeles in the fall to pursue a degree in either communications or sports medicine. "A lot of doors have opened up that I never really expected," she says. "But I have to keep my feet on the ground. Education is really important to me and my family. [Her father is a heart surgeon.] I need to get back to school. I'll do the best I can, but the tour is going to have to fit into my schedule. I need to be a normal college student. I'm eighteen. I need to get on to the next chapter in my life."

At UCLA Kerri plans to participate in the gymnastics program, although she won't compete for the university. "I'll go to the competitions and help them with other aspects of the program."

All in all, Kerri is philosophical about her future. "It's fortunate that it's all worked out so smoothly. Initially I faced a lot of hard decisions. But now I know what I'm going to do."

Her short-term goals, besides attending college, are completing the tour with her teammates and making promotional appearances. "But right now I'm just

Kerri stuck her second vault landing despite her injured ankle.

enjoying being at home and doing fun things, being with my family and friends. I'll deal with everything else when the time comes."

Having won the team gold medal after years of training, hard work, and sacrifice, Kerri says that what she loves most about being a gymnast is "the satisfaction I get when I do something well, or when I worked really hard to get something, and didn't get it and didn't get it, and finally got it."

Now Kerri is an American champion and a role model for thousands of young fans who will look up to her the way she once looked up to Mary Lou Retton. "It's a great feeling when little kids say, 'I want to be just like you!' It puts things into perspective. Everyone is focusing on 'You're an Olympic champion,' but it's a lot more than that. We are representing our sport. We have a larger role to play."

Duomo/David Madison

In terrible pain from her badly sprained ankle, Kerri crawled off the mat at the 1996 Olympics.

Kerri could not compete in the individuals at the Olympics, but she may have achieved enough dreams for a lifetime. After all, she's an American gold medal champion, now and forever.

THE MAGNIFICENT SEVEN

Doug Pensinger/AllSport

Kerri's coach, Bela Karolyi, carried the injured champion off the podium after the 1996 Olympic team gold medals had been awarded.

★ KERRI STRUG

FAN MAIL ADDRESSES
FOR TEAM USA

AMANDA BORDEN
Cincinnati Gymnastics
3330 Port Union Road
Fairfield, OH 45014

AMY CHOW
West Valley
1190 Dell Avenue, Unit #1
Campbell, CA 95008

DOMINIQUE DAWES
Hill's Angels
7557 Lindbergh Drive
Gaithersburg, MD 20879

SHANNON MILLER
P.O. Box 5103
Edmond, OK 73083-5103

DOMINIQUE MOCEANU
P.O. Box 90908
Houston, TX 77290-0908

JAYCIE PHELPS
Cincinnati Gymnastics
3330 Port Union Road
Fairfield, OH 45014

KERRI STRUG
P.O. Box 34B
Balboa Island, CA 92662

USA GYMNASTICS INFORMATION

USA Gymnastics is the sole national governing body (NGB) for the sport of gymnastics in the United States. It gets this designation from the International Olympic Committee and the International Gymnastics Federation. USA Gymnastics sets the rules and policies that govern gymnastics in this country. Training and selecting the U.S. Gymnastics Teams for the Olympics and World Championships are just two of the many responsibilities of USA Gymnastics. For additional information on USA Gymnastics and its events, contact the main office at (317) 237-5050; for membership call 1-800-345-4719; for merchandise call 1-800-4USA GYM. And visit USA Gymnastics on the World Wide Web at http://www.usa-gymnastics.org/usag/.

Published by
Bantam Books
Bantam Doubleday Dell Publishing Group, Inc.
1540 Broadway
New York, New York 10036

Nancy H. Kleinbaum is a journalist who has written numerous novelizations.

Self-end photograph Gene Stafford 1996/Courtesy of Shade Global
All baby photographs courtesy of gymnasts' families

Bantam Books are published by Bantam Books, a division of Bantam Doubleday Dell Publishing Group, Inc. Its trademark, consisting of the words "Bantam Books" and the portrayal of a rooster, is Registered in U.S. Patent and Trademark Office and in other countries. Marca Registrada.

Library of Congress Cataloging-in-Publication Data
ISBN: 0-553-09774-1
Cataloging-in-Publication Data is available from the U.S. Library of Congress.
The text of this book is set in 14-point Adobe Garamond.
Book design by Susan Clark Dominguez
Manufactured in the United States of America
October 1996
10 9 8 7 6 5 4 3 2 1